HALBRITTER'S ARMOURY

*An introduction to the secret weapons of history
from the fortresses of ancient Egypt
to the flying machines of the nineteenth century.
With many illustrations specially drawn
for the book by its compiler.*

Translated by Jamie Muir

Halbritter's Armoury

An introduction to the secret weapons of history

Ernest Benn
LONDON & TONBRIDGE

First published in Germany 1977 by
Carl Hanser Verlag.

First published in Great Britain 1978 by
Ernest Benn Limited.
25 New Street Square, London EC4 3JA.
and Sovereign Way, Tonbridge, Kent TN9 1RW.

© *1977 Carl Hanser Verlag München Wien.*
English Translation ©*1978 Jamie Muir.*

Printed in Great Britain by Balding & Mansell Ltd.
ISBN 0 510 00039-8

Introductory Note

What distinguishes this book from all other histories of
weaponry is that it principally examines an aspect of the
subject hitherto unexplored: design failure. And in
particular the failure in design of secret weaponry from
Antiquity to the present day.

The book has taken many years of extensive, privately-
funded research and though it cannot claim to be a catalogue
raisonée of all such weapons it does aim to examine wherever
possible the basic prototype rather than its multitudinous
variants.

The author presumes that his readers do not wish to be bored
by measurements and specifications, nor by the quot-
ation of sources.

The Spartan Ram, later The Rabbit Punch

Fortresses existed in ancient Greece and even then special devices were required to attack them. The Spartan Ram was popular because of its simple, inexpensive construction. During the Swabian War of 1499 the enemies of the Swabian Federation modelled their battering rams in the shapes of rabbits after hearing that no animal struck more terror in the Swabian heart.

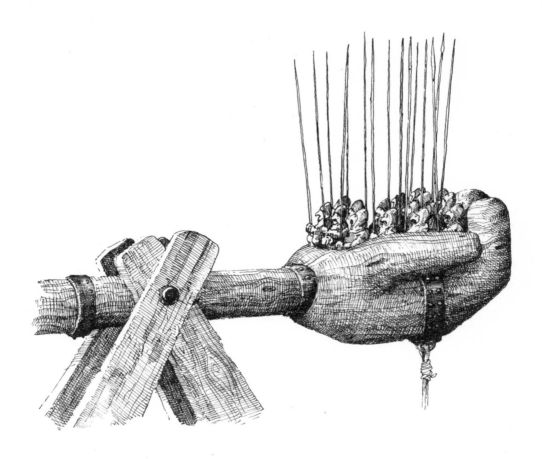

The Hand Grenade

The Hand Grenade was carved out of hard wood bound with iron bands and counter-weighted with a single granite boulder. It was much used in ancient times but the Roman authorities phased it out because of the extraordinarily high injury rate amongst Hand Grenadiers.

The War Horse

This is one of the earliest known examples of mechanised weaponry. During the rule of the tyrants Hippias and Hipparch (527-514 B.C.) the War Horse was often used for street fighting. The complicated way in which it moved made daily exercises obligatory.

The Duck

Between 483-481 the Romans built and launched one hundred and eighty amphibious craft, This was the first historically-recorded fleet building programme. Of course this type of craft has antecedents in legend, one such exists in the Old Testament (cf. The Book of Jonah.)

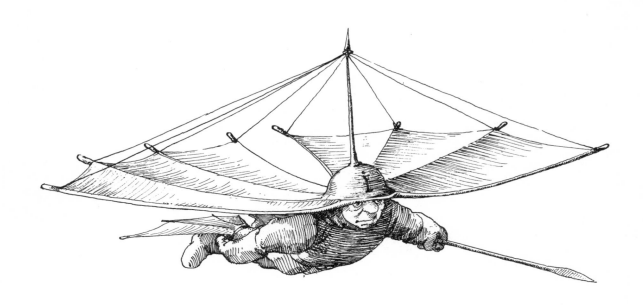

Grecian Hang Gliders

The account of the escape of Daedalus and Icarus from the Labyrinth at Knossos was an inspiration to the weapons industry of the day despite the tragic outcome of Icarus's test flight.

Flying Helmet F 104, shown above, was considered extremely difficult to fly by those chosen to wear it.

Nevertheless in battle the Grecian Hang Gliders were thought to be unbeatable.

Double-spread illustration overleaf: manoeuvres, late summer, 400 B.C.

The Thunder Barrel

This classic example of design failure lead to the decisive defeat of the Spartans at the battle of Leuktra. The introduction of the Hoplite formation permitted the Roman ranks to part well before the Thunder Barrels reached them, the barrels rolling past harmlessly to shatter on the rocks below.

19

Tactical Weaponry

Homer, the eighth-century Greek, in the Iliad was the first man to describe the cunning use of a wooden horse at the siege of Troy. Other tactical weapons of equal ingenuity may have been used, but if they were the Greeks to this day are keeping the details secret and no plans are available to reproduce above.

Inflatable Cohorts (Sleeping Beauties)

Prisoners in state prisons were set the task of stitching together goatskins which, when painted, looked like a soldier asleep. These Inflatable Cohorts or Sleeping Beauties as they became popularly known, were positioned in front of an enemy fortress to give the impression of a sleeping army. The strategy had unexpected results—both the besiegers and the besieged fell asleep.

Disc-Throwers: Grecian and Roman

The technique of disc-throwing became famous throughout the Ancient World as Greek culture spread after the conquests of Alexander the Great. The music the spinning discs made when hurled into the air was particularly pleasing and the legions of Rome could not resist lending an ear to its tunes.

The Tortoise or Testudo

Pyrrhus's victory against the Romans at the Slaughter of Ausculum in 279 B.C. was, to a large extent, the result of his skilful use of twenty-six armoured cavalry elephants, a strategy which had resounding consequences. Armies everywhere rushed to equip themselves and even cats and dogs were armour-plated although animals with naturally thick skins were more readily convertible.

An Athenian Missile Battery (With Homer Device)

The failure of the Athenians to liberate themselves from the
Macedonian occupying forces in 265 B.C. is, according to the
author's research, largely attributable to their dilletante use
of missiles with untested and, as far as aim was concerned,
almost irresponsibly inaccurate warheads.

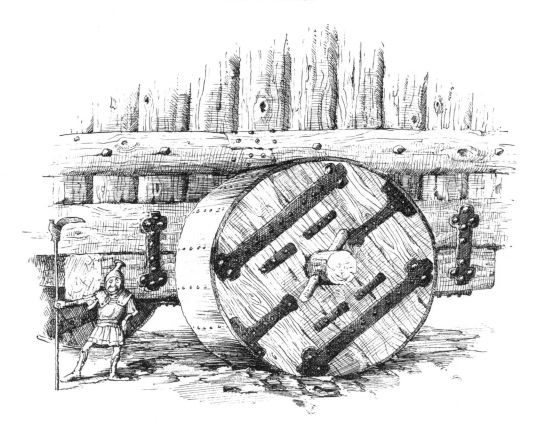

The Lobster Pot, A Mobile Prisoner of War Camp

The invasion of Roman territory by Celts hell-bent on freeing themselves from the yoke of Rome necessitated the invention of mobile prisoner of war camps colloquially known as Lobster Pots.

The strategy was a simple one. The Romans left the gates of these forts ajar, to tempt the Celts inside, and concealed themselves in nearby undergrowth. The approaching Celts seeing the forts unguarded rushed inside, whereupon the Romans broke cover and slammed the gates shut from the outside. As a result several thousand Celts were towed into captivity between the years 133-179 B.C.

**A Stately Subquinquereme with its Bamboo Snorkels
in the "Up" Position**

One of the little known facts of history is that the conquest of
Carthage in 146 B.C. was largely decided by the Subquinquereme. Surprisingly one hundred years later this
miracle weapon was already obsolescent and only brought
out to intimidate visiting heads of state.

The Carthaginian Stork Squadron

Carthaginian attempts to gain air
supremacy in the Spring Offensive of 146 B.C.
failed because of the unreliability
of the Stork Squadron.
The Squadron had to follow the migratory
pattern of its storks and scrambled
at no other time.

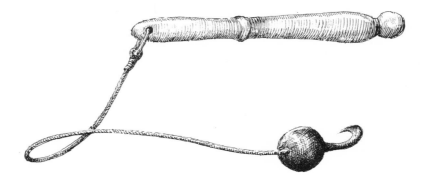

Kamikazi Catapulters

Caesar's legions came face to face with Kamikazi Catapulters for the first time when the Gauls led by Vercingetorix rebelled. They catapulted themselves over the walls of Roman fortresses by an ingenious, if suicidal, method.

The Bomber Eagle

Caesar's crossing of the Rubicon, his pursuit of Pompey, the conquest of Spain and other victories could never have been achieved without the stone bombs made by Gallic blacksmiths and dropped on Caesar's enemies by squadrons of specially trained eagles. However, it is one of the ironies of history that Caesar's undoubted supremacy in the air was powerless to protect him from his friends on the ground. Despite this (or perhaps because of it) the eagle has become the insignia of emperors.

The Baconeers

The decline and fall of the Roman Empire was considerably hastened by the Baconeers, most feared of all the northern hordes. To call the Baconeers a fighting unit is to presume they understood military discipline. They did not. Their only motivation was greed. Pillage and rape they regarded with keen anticipation. Therefore although the Visigothic High Command appreciated their ferocity it was continually at a loss to know how to keep the Baconeers in check. They had an unattractive habit of butchering anyone sent to command them.

43

Thorn Armour

The military advantage of the infantryman has often been demonstrated throughout history. Thorn Armour was devised to give him 360° protection, but it never proved popular. Once the infantryman had been encased in the armour he was powerless to remove it.

The Glove Dagger
The Glove Dagger was one of a number of weapons devised to tackle the Thorn Armour battalions. The above is a reproduction of the only known example of this particular weapon, which was dug out of a pit near the Milvian bridge.

A Two-Hander

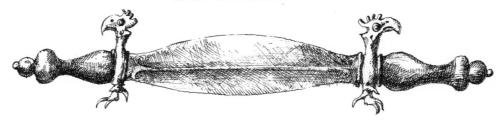

A Thumb-Saw

Hand to Hand Combat

The demands of hand to hand combat led to a vast number of different types of weapon. Lack of space regrettably prevents us from illustrating more than a few examples. The shape of these weapons, their uses and, less often, the names of their inventors survive in their technical terminology.

An Ankle-Slasher

A Cheek-Hook

A Double Cheek-Hook

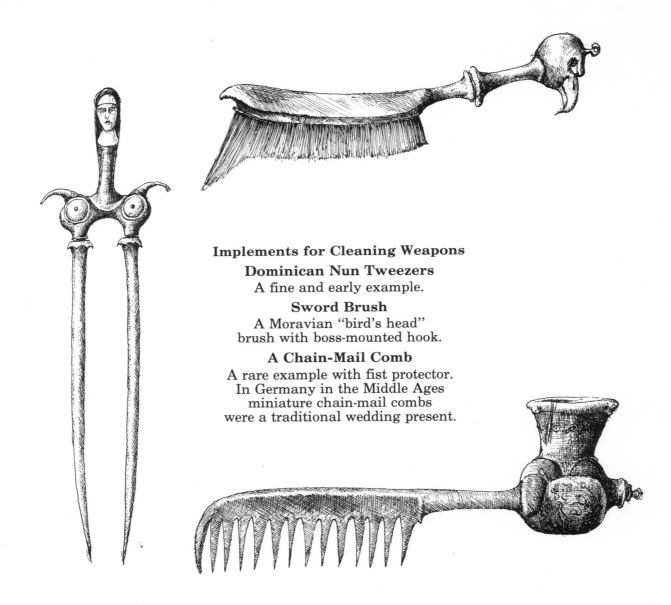

Implements for Cleaning Weapons

Dominican Nun Tweezers
A fine and early example.

Sword Brush
A Moravian "bird's head"
brush with boss-mounted hook.

A Chain-Mail Comb
A rare example with fist protector.
In Germany in the Middle Ages
miniature chain-mail combs
were a traditional wedding present.

Adolph "Cheeks" Rundse
The double cheek-hook was named after him.
father, "Helpful" Rundse the Elder is credited with
the invention of the single blade cheek-hook.

Hans "Camel Hair" Herrlich
Three hundred and ninety-eight sword brushes made by his
own hands exist today.

The Terror Bell

By 391 A.D. Christianity had established itself as the state religion of the greater part of the known world and new forms of weaponry were proving popular. One new development was the Terror Bell which demoralised attacking armies by its persistent clanging. Note the steel cadaver scoop, an intriguing design modification of the 390's.

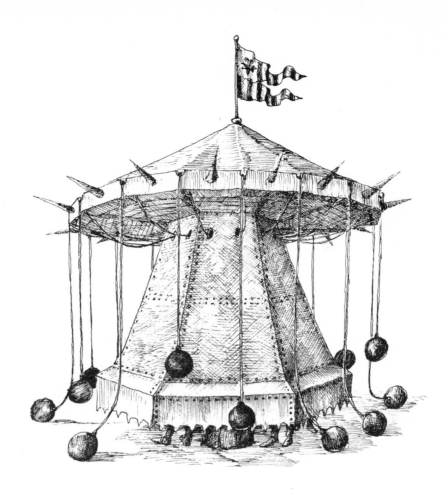

The Merry-Go-Wound

The effectiveness of this weapon depended upon the enemy mistaking it for an harmless fairground Merry-Go-Round. When it was approached to within striking distance, mechanics hidden from sight inside the central core revolved the Merry-Go-Wound at high speed. The iron balls suspended from the deceptively ornamental canopy flew outwards and severely wounded the enemy.

However, the weapon was extraordinarily expensive to produce, not readily transportable, and its distinctive appearance made avoidance a simple and wholly effective tactic.

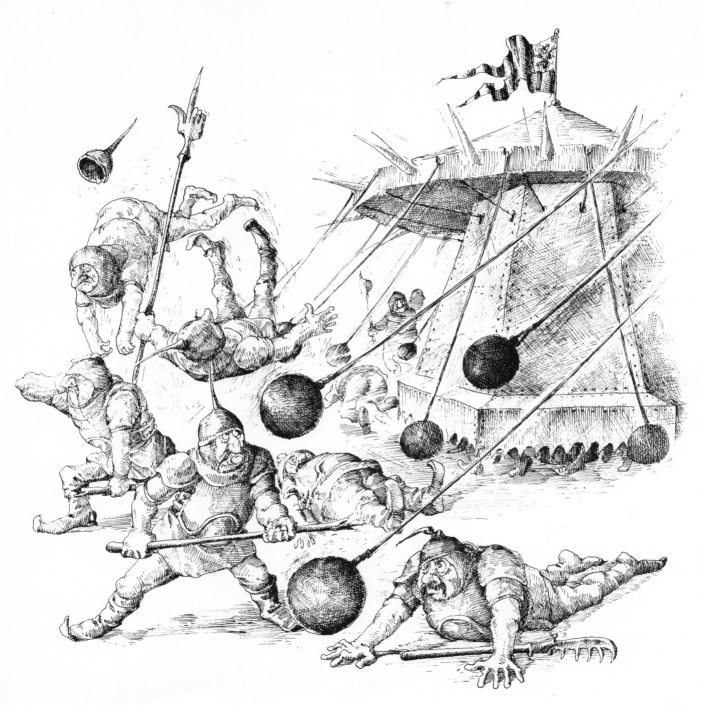

Pitch-Pipers

The siege remained a popular method of waging war throughout the Middle-Ages. Special weapons were devised to storm castles and the besieged often displayed equal ingenuity in repelling attacks. The illustration on the opposite page is an example of the inventiveness of the military mind *in extremis*.

The commander of the fortress at Pochlarn lost so many of his troops to the Bavarian black palsy that he was forced to press into service the brass section of his army band. The illustration shows the loading and discharging of what proved to be viciously effective—globules of boiling pitch trumpeted onto the heads of the enemy.

The Field Screw

The Field Screw was one of a number of weapons devised to pierce enemy defences. Under cover of night whole sections of palisade could be removed (see illustration) and sentries on guard duty were trained to listen out for the faint rhythmical squeak of an enemy Field Screw working its way into their wooden fortifications.

Gunpowder

Just who it was who invented gunpowder is a subject much
debated amongst historians but recent research conducted
by the author of this work proves conclusively that the
inventor was a quiet, unassuming Bernardine monk called
Brother Bertold Schwarz. Uncertain of what use he might
make of his discovery Brother Bertold took his powder to
demonstrate to a fellow monk. The quotations are from a
contemporary eye-witness account:

"Saltpetre, sulphur, charcoal,
Saltpetre, sulphur, charcoal,
Saltpetre . . ."

"My name is Brother Bertold Schwarz."

"What can I do for you?"

"Well, I've invented this powder."

"Oh yes, what's it for?"

"Well if you'll let me borrow your ink-pot
I'll give you a demonstration."

"I must say I'm curious to know what it does."

"Its use I dedicate to God."

"Fine, but what's the point of it?"

"Now, you hold it firmly while I make a
spark with my tinderbox."

"This is absolutely fascinating."

"Bang!"

"Saltpetre, sulphur, charcoal—that's all you need!"
"Well yes, perhaps, but I still can't see
that there is going to be much use for it . . ."

The Pottery Bomb

The invention of gunpowder changed the nature of warfare completely, yet it was some time before an efficient use could be found for Brother Bertold's invention. To begin with gunpowder was merely poured into earthenware receptacles which were then ignited in the path of an advancing army. These pottery bombs exploded with a loud bang; they were not dangerous except occasionally to those lighting them.

The Pepper Bellows

Pepper first became known in Europe after the Dutch discovered the East Indies. At the time it was a fairly widely held belief that pepper, rather than gunpowder, would revolutionise warfare. Unfortunately the designer of the tactical Pepper Bellows failed to take into consideration the disastrous effect of a prevailing wind upon the army operating it, and production was swiftly discontinued.

As a result, pepper went out of favour with armament manufacturers. Which explains why in histories of warfare so much has been written about gunpowder and so little about pepper.

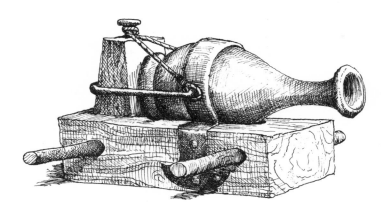

The Invention of the Cannon

The cannon was invented accidentally by a simple blacksmith called Frederick Wuchtel who came from the town of Eisenberg in eastern Germany. Wuchtel was in the habit of keeping a quantity of powder in his smithy sealed inside a metal container. One day Wuchtel forgot to replace the top. He realised his mistake almost immediately and thrust it back but he was too late. A spark from the forge had ignited the powder and, with a violent explosion, the top of the container was blown through the smithy roof. Wuchtel, badly shaken, looked up to where his predecessor, an Englishman, had engraved an inscription, part in English, part in Latin: "Oh Lorde admitte meus fore I can non existe sine teus". The missile had torn away the words "can non".

"Whatever it is that I have invented", said Wuchtel pointing to the hole in his roof, "it shall henceforth be called the can non".

69

The Muzzle-Loading Haversack Five Pounder

The demonstration of this new weapon was one of a number of festivities arranged to celebrate the coronation of Ferdinand I as king of Bohemia and Hungary. But the ballistics experts responsible for the design failed to take into account the effect of recoil; it was said at the time that had the gun not been blessed it might have dethroned the Emperor or worse.

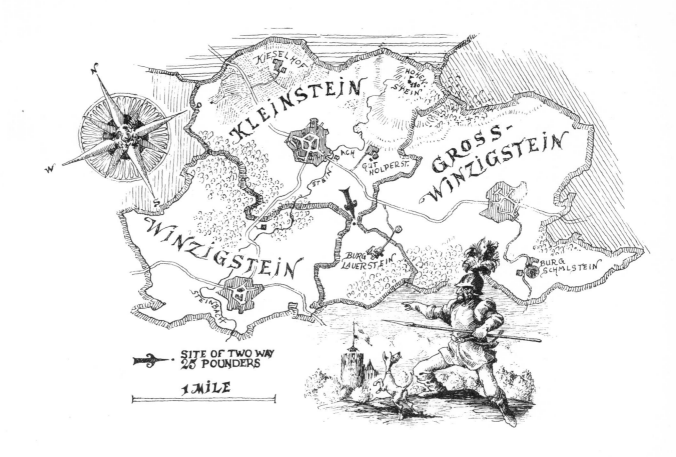

The Two-Way Twenty-Five Pounder

Until it became unified after the Reformation, Germany was a mass of small states whose rulers were perpetually at war with each other. Alliances seemed to exist only to be broken and because one never knew which of one's neighbours were friendly and which hostile, the two-way twenty-five pounder was a particularly useful weapon. Fired from high ground, the cannon could subjugate two enemy armies approaching simultaneously from either North and South, or from East and West, or from North-North West and South-South East, or from North-North West by West and South-South East by East . . .

An Episcopal Pistol

Unfortunately this work can only deal superficially with the religious wars of the sixteenth century. But in passing the reader should note that the True Faith was hammered home with ferocious zeal by the field curates of both persuasions, who often accompanied cavalry charges using a number of specially designed hand weapons.

Papal Galleons
These stately craft proclaimed the religious message of the
Papacy by their sheer size and impressiveness.

The Conquest of the Americas by the Trojan Duck
The conquest of the Americas could not have been
accomplished without Trojan Ducks. Their size so terrified
the native Indians that they fled in horror before them and
the roar of their beak-mounted cannon became known as the
"quack of doom".

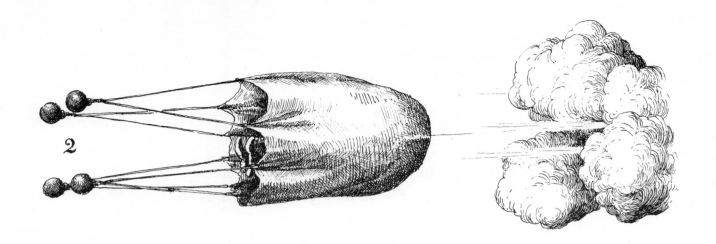

The First Airborne Infantry

The Italian painter and inventor
Leonardo da Vinci discovered the
principles governing both powered
flight and the parachute but the latter
seemed to the arms industry of the
High Renaissance to be pointless
without the practical realisation of
the former—i.e. a soldier had to be up
in the air before he could hope to
parachute down upon an enemy.
The illustrations depict one ill-fated
method devised to overcome this
problem:
1. A four-barrelled cannon (a)
2. shot an infantryman (b) strapped
into a weighted parachute (c) and
armed with an axe with which to cut
himself free (d) over enemy lines.
3. Landing was a nightmare which
few survived.

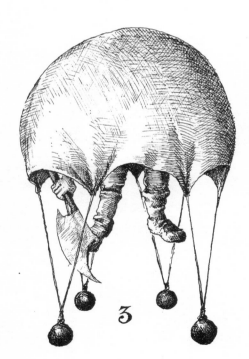

The Hog Mortar
When Emperor Charles V's political and military power was at its peak his easily manoeuvred batteries of Hog Mortars were even more feared than the Spanish cavalry.
1. Taking aim.
2. Rolling out the gun carriage.
3. A sniff of grapeshot.

Itching Powder

Another alternative to gunpowder, once as seriously considered as pepper, was itching powder. An anonymous mendicant monk from Worms invented a type which had to be activated on the battlefield by contact with running water. But the effervescing powder produced an incurable desire to itch in both armies and research was abandoned.

A Hothead Charging into Battle

As the Age of the Bow and Arrow gave way to the Age of
Gunpowder a band of elderly knights formed together to
combine the time-honoured chivalric ideals of honour and
fortitude with the new technology of gunpowder and cannon.
Younger men saluted their brave but reckless gesture by
nick-naming them The Hotheads. It was not wise for old men
to charge into battle beneath the weight of a recoiling
howitzer and all but one of The Hotheads perished in their
first encounter with the enemy.

An Old Bohemian Keg Helmet
Worn by auxiliary troops recruited from the monasteries, Keg Helmets were easily recognisable at a distance and served as a useful badge of rank.

An Iron Maiden Helmet
This helmet came in different shapes and sizes but always denoted absolute matrimonial fidelity on the part of the officer beneath.

A Ceremonial Cocked Hat
These emblems of masculinity were donned by a raffish element amongst the Bohemian army to mock the solemn fidelity of those who perspired beneath the weight of the Iron Maiden.

An Old Frankish Thumb Helmet
The example shown here with protective ear flaps was hugely popular throughout the Middle Ages.

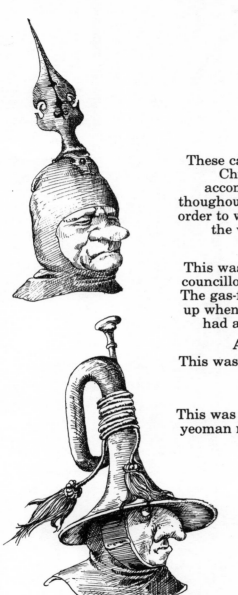

A Quill Pen Cap

These caps were the emblem of the Chronicler Division, who accompanied military leaders thoughout the seventeenth century in order to write up their heroic deeds in the very best possible light.

A Bulb Hat

This was a symbol of rank amongst councillors both of war and of peace. The gas-filled balloon of white felt lit up whenever the attached councillor had a particularly bright idea.

A Trumpet Helmet.

This was adopted by musicians of the Music Corps.

A Snail Cap

This was worn by the rearguard of the yeoman regiments, mostly old men of humble origins.

The Tree Helmet Battalion

The Age of Reason had a profound influence upon the
history of warfare, deception and trickery became weapons
as powerful as gunpowder and the cannon. The illustration
above shows a soldier of the Tree Helmet Battalion which
seized a number of castles by disguising itself as an orchard.
The tactic remained successful until the enemy developed a
powerful defoliant.

Ducking Under
The military man's proverbial love of animals was exploited
by teams of powerful swimmers who captured a number of
moated castles in this underhand, underwater way.

A Chinese Delegation Shabbily Treated

Even in the seventeenth century diplomacy was a dangerous business. Although most nations recognised the important part it played ·in the prevention of war, the concept of diplomatic immunity simply did not exist. On one occasion, after a delegation of Chinese had revealed some valuable information at an embassy reception, they were stabbed in the back by a murderous device adorning the helmets of the Bulgarian servants detailed to look after them.

Bladed Breastplates

A large number of officers went into the Thirty Years War in the belief that it would be over by Christmas 1618. At home their wives became more and more furious as the years passed by. By 1648 many officers simply could not face the anger of their spouses and returned home wearing Bladed Breastplates. These ensured that homecomings were brief and to the point and lengthy explanations superfluous.

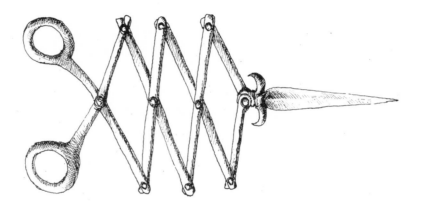

The Scissor Stabber

The wives of soldiers fighting in the Thirty Years War had to rely upon the resourcefulness of their servants to protect them from the bands of marauding mercenaries who roamed throughout Europe. Out of everyday implements an astonishing variety of weapons were constructed (see above.)

The Glove Clout

By the seventeenth century the art of The Joust had degenerated badly. Whereas in the Middle Ages noble knights had tilted against each other for a lady's favour, in the sixteen-eighties crowds would gather to watch a couple of roughs glove clouting for a pig.

Castles, Forts and Fortifications

Defence being as much a part of warfare as attack the author
of the present work has seen fit to include here a short
digression on the subject.

Egyptian Sand Castles
The sand dunes in the North African desert are all that remains of the extensive system of Egyptian built sand fortifications.
On the opposite page: Tutankhamen's Wall. One of the Wonders of the World which collapsed before it could be numbered.

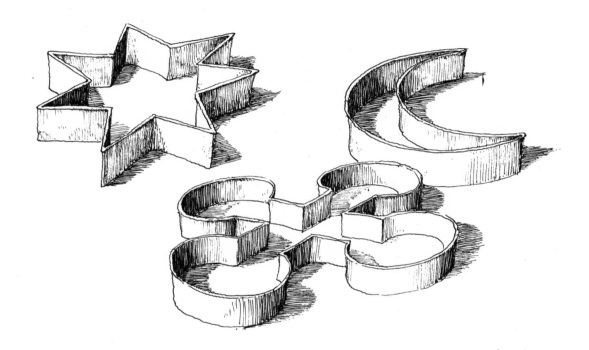

Biscuit Forts

Leonardo da Vinci, Albrecht Dürer and Sebastian de Vauban are the best known names in the history of forts and fortifications. Less well known is the work of Hans George Blech, the son of a bricklayer, whose constructions appear to have been based on seventeenth century biscuit moulds.

Digression: Castle Building

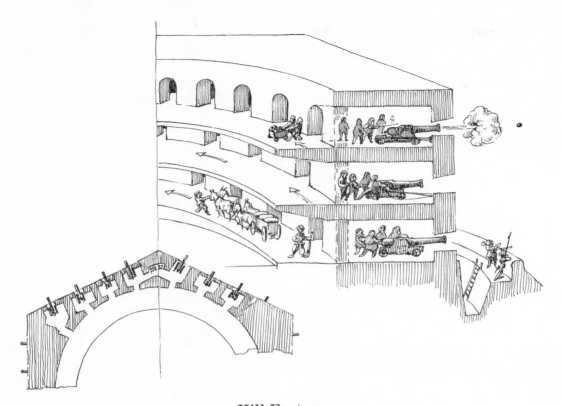

Hill Fortresses
Above: **Section and Plan of a Nüt Fortress** (see overleaf)

Opposite page: **Half Moon Fortress**

Page 112. **A view of the Nüt Fortresses protecting the important trading town of Bölt in northern Germany.**

Page 113. **A map of Bölt and the surrounding Nüts.**

Page 114. **A Mexican Sombrero Fort.**

Page 115. **A Castle on the Toe of Italy.**

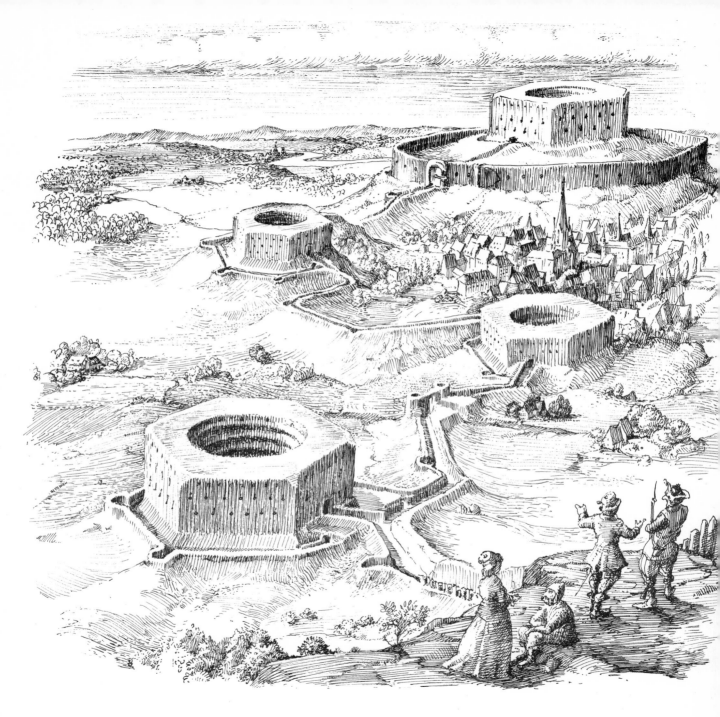

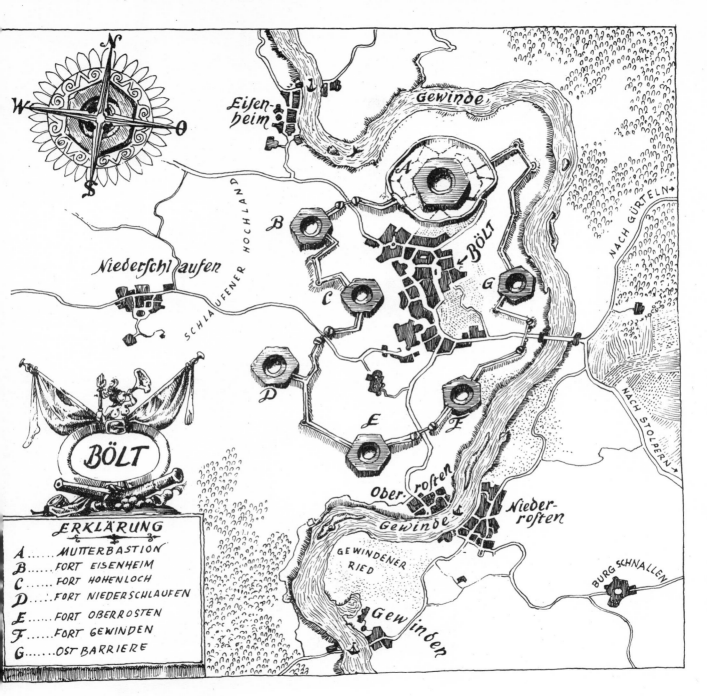

BÖLT

ERKLÄRUNG

A .... MUTTERBASTION
B .... FORT EISENHEIM
C .... FORT HOHENLOCH
D .... FORT NIEDERSCHLAUFEN
E .... FORT OBERROSTEN
F .... FORT GEWINDEN
G .... OST BARRIERE

Phoney Forts

Phoney Forts were first erected by Russian princes in the later part of the seventeenth century to intimidate their neighbours, an early example of psychological warfare. After a tour of these impressive but entirely bogus fortifications neighbouring heads of state were so demoralised they invariably signed wholly disadvantageous peace treaties.

Some Seventeenth Century Developments In The Science Of Gunnery.

The Up and Over Twenty Pounder

This cannon enabled armies to fire over walls and other major obstructions in the field. The Up and Over came with a number of different barrel lengths and a cunning modification which enabled it to fire round corners.

The Parthian Pounder

It has been said more than once that the best form of attack is defence, for an army is never more vulnerable than at the moment it senses victory. Disciplined formations are abandoned, the infantry rush forward impetuously and the Parthian Pounder comes into its own. It was a devastating weapon which more than once completely reversed the almost certain outcome of a battle. Note the more intimate Parthian Arquebus in the foreground of the double-spread overleaf.

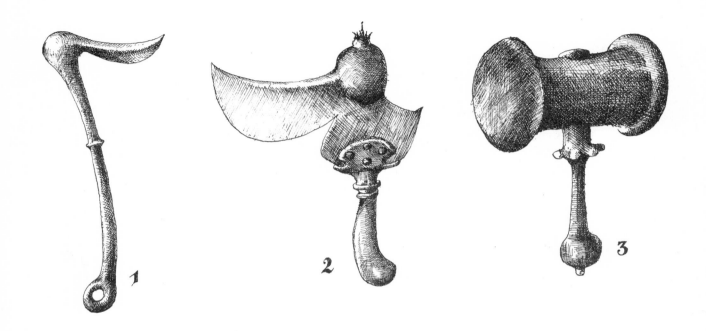

A Muscovy Hook (1)   **A Mandarin Axe** (2)   **A Mallard Mallet** (3)

In an attempt to diminish the infantryman's fear of hand-to-hand combat, arms manufacturers conceived the idea of naming their weapons after harmless ducks. A ploy which fooled no-one.

A Ramming Galley (male version with submerged ram.)

A female version also existed. (see overleaf.)

Imperial Cannon Crackers

More often than not The Holy Roman Empire's Cannon Crackers were operated by dispossessed Moldavian small-holders. Opposite page: the seizing of a twenty-five pounder. Note the navigator seated beneath the helmet cupola. Note, too, the formal grace and discipline of the Moldavians.

The Sauerkraut War

Every school boy knows about the Sauerkraut War but few people know of the great Cabbage Controversy of 1479 which led to it. Half Germany believed that broad-leafed cabbages made the best sauerkraut, the other half championed the cause of the narrow-leaf cabbage. The war which followed was fought with (A) The Two-Handed Cabbage Shredder, (B) The Vinegar Sprinkler, (C) The Sauerkraut Shovel.

The Hornberg Engagement

First Day: 3rd October, afternoon 14.25. The men of Hornberg and their opponents, the men of Villing, attempt to confuse each other by bold circling movements.

Second Day: 4th October, 10.15. The men of Hornberg and their opponents after a mid-morning break start yesterday's operations all over again.

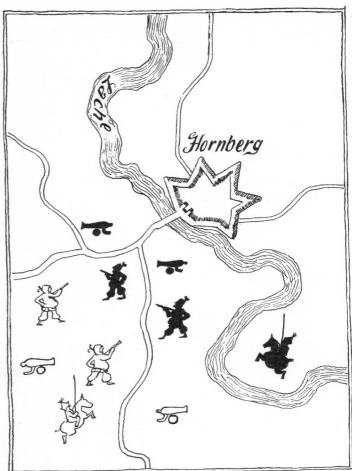

Third Day: 5th October, morning 4.45. After early mass the men of Hornberg and their opponents attempt to force a decision by a night battle.

Third Day: 5th October, afternoon 17.30. The men of Hornberg and their opponents reconquer their initial positions and, had they not all died of old age, they would still be fighting today.

Small Arms

The Spiral Musket
The spiralled barrel of this ingenious weapon gave it a potent muzzle velocity and its periscopic sights enabled a fusilier to fire from behind complete cover. Much loved throughout the eighteenth century.

Small Arms

A Cross-Country Arquebus
Considerably less ingenious than the Spiral Musket,
the Cross-Country Arquebus was cumbersome and not
at all accurate.

Breastworks

The method of defence known as Breastworks was introduced onto the continent during the seventeenth century by a military tactician who had observed similar defences protecting the city of Bristol during the English Civil War (1642-1648).

135

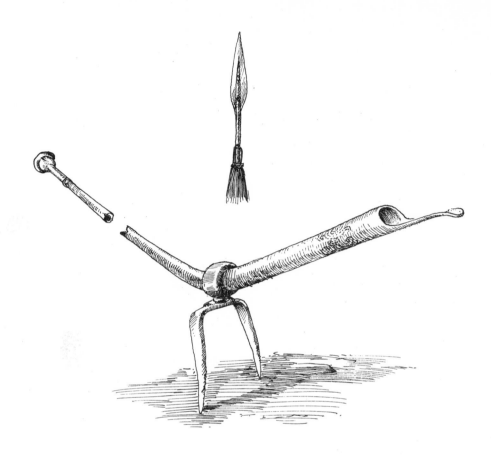

The Blowpipes of St. Blaise

The legendary invincibility of alpine fortresses was in no small part due to the blowpipers of St. Blaise who rained down volley after volley of steel-tipped darts upon their enemies. Subsequent generations of Swiss failed to understand that the St. Blaise blowpipe was a weapon of war and not a musical instrument.

The Iron Gustav

Nineteenth century antiquarian passion for the Middle Ages almost went too far in Lippe-Detmold. An arms manufacturer there seriously considered reintroducing the faintly obscene Iron Gustav, a suit of armour with drop hatch cod-piece and multiple loading cannon. But both the Health and the Education authorities intervened and the manufacturer was forced to cancel production. Even in the Middle Ages the Iron Gustav was always considered below the belt.

Nineteenth Century

A Foot Soldier
The foot soldier was the backbone of any army. In the
illustration on the opposite page a squad receives
special duty instruction: how to get (a) into (b).

a   *b*

141

An Army Canteen

The introduction in the nineteenth century of regimental mascots, ornate chest medals, elaborate flags and fancy weapons proves how peaceful the century was. An army that has no one to fight redesigns its uniforms.

A Swiss Card
Following the example of the Pope
many princelings of the Church
engaged ceremonial guards who,
when they were not asleep, spent
their time playing cards.

The Belly Corps
Veteran troops with enormous paunches were conscripted into a Corps de Belly which paraded as a warning to others not to shirk their duties.

145

Sirens
Swiss women found lucrative employment throughout
Europe as part of the Early Warning System. Opposite page:
note powerful lungs.

Garden Warfare
Many princes employed troops ostensibly to dig defensive trenches, but the sappers often found themselves excavating baroque gardens in the french manner instead.

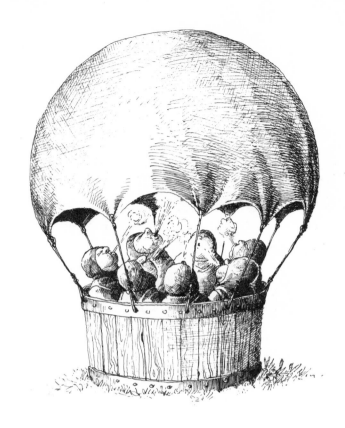

The War in the Air

Two thousand five hundred years after the first flights of the Grecian Hang Gliders (see page 14) military inventors returned once again to the idea of aerial warfare. The Sky Tub should have been borne aloft by the powerful puffing of its pilots but it never once left the ground. More successful was a later model which rose to a height of several feet. Herons yoked to the tub were supposed to tow it across land and sea but they had a tendency to peck at the balloon fabric. Because of this the Sky Tub pilots, who were affectionately nick-named the Heron Folk, tended to be men of extraordinary courage and insensitivity.

Hot Pantaloons

Hot Pantaloons were designed to provide common soldiers with the manoeuvrability they needed so vitally. Hot air from the bellows warmed the privates in cold weather but the brow wings were tiring to operate and the corks had a tendency to pop out in mid-flight. Laughed at by their fellow infantrymen, shot at by the enemy, one must salute the bravery of these martyrs to design folly.

153

An Introduction to the Secret Weapons of History

Index

A

Adolph "Cheeks" Rundse 49
Ankle-Slasher 47
Army Canteen 142-143
Athenian Missile Battery 30-31

B

Baconeers 42-43
Belly Corps 145
Biscuit Forts 108-109
Bladed Breastplates 98-99
Blowpipes of St. Blaise 136-137
Bomber Eagle 40-41
Breastworks 134-135
Bulb Hat 91

C

Castle on the Toe of Italy 115
Castles, Forts and Fortifications 105
Carthaginian Stork Squadron 35
Ceremonial Cocked Hat 90
Chain-Mail Comb 48
Cheek-Hook 47
Chinese Delegation Shabbily Treated 96-97
Conquest of the Americas by the Trojan Duck 80-81
Cross-Country Arquebus 133

D

Disc-Throwers 26-27
Dominican Nun Tweezers 48
Double Cheek-Hook 47
Duck 12-13
Ducking Under 94-95

E

Egyptian Sand Castles 106-107
Episcopal Pistol 76-77

F

Field Screw 56-57
First Airborne Infantry 82-83
Foot Soldier 140-141

G

Garden Warfare 148-149
Glove Clout 102-103
Glove Dagger 45
Grecian Hang Gliders 14-17
Gunpowder 58-62

H

Half-Moon Fortress 110
Hand Grenade 8-9
Hand to Hand Combat 46
Hans "Camel Hair" Herrlich 49
Hog Mortar 84-85
Hornberg Engagement 130-131
Hothead Charging into Battle 88-89
Hot Pantaloons 152-153

I

Imperial Cannon Crackers 126-127
Implements for Cleaning Weapons 48
Inflatable Cohorts 23-25
Invention of the Canon 68-69
Iron Gustav 138-139
Iron Maiden Helmet 90
Itching Powder 86-87

K

Kamikazi Catapulters 36-39

L

Lobster Pot 32-33

M

Mallard Mallet 122
Mandarin Axe 122
Merry-Go-Wound 52-53
Mexican Sombrero Fort 114
Muscovy Hook 122
Muzzle-Loading Haversack
   Five Pounder 70-73

N

Nüt Fortresses 111-113

O

Old Bohemian Keg Helmet
   90
Old Frankish Thumb Helmet
   90

P

Papal Galleons 78-79
Parthian Pounder 120-121
Pepper Bellows 66-67
Phoney Forts 116-117
Pitch Pipers 54-55
Pottery Bomb 63-65

Q

Quill Pen Cap 91

R

Ramming Galley 123
Ramming Galley (female
   version) 124

S

Sauerkraut War, The 128-129
Scissor Stabber 100-101
Sirens 146-147
Small Arms 132-133
Snail Cap 91
Spartan Ram 6-7
Spiral Musket 132
Stately Subquinquereme 34
Swiss Card 144
Sword Brush 48

T

Tactical Weaponry 22
Terror Bell 50-51
Thorn Armour 44
Thumb-Saw 46
Thunder Barrel 18-21
Tortoise or Testudo 28-29
Tree Helmet Battalion 92-93
Trumpet Helmet 91
Two-Hander 46
Two-Way Twenty-five
   Pounder 74-75

U

Up and Over Twenty
   Pounder 118-119

W

War Horse 10-11
War in the Air 150-151